The Salt and the Song

The Salt and the Song

Virginia Petrucci

HEADMISTRESS PRESS

ISBN: 978-0-9995930-6-6

Cover art by Romaine Brooks, *Ida Rubinstein* 1917 Public Domain.
Cover & book design by Mary Meriam.

PUBLISHER
Headmistress Press
60 Shipview Lane
Sequim, WA 98382
Telephone: 917-428-8312
Email: headmistresspress@gmail.com
Website: headmistresspress.blogspot.com

Table of Contents

How the Ocean

How often is looking seeing?

A she, no doubt
laps puddleless about
the people who title her Ocean

A sexless water we want to shemonize
(and yet)

Water like a sphere as defined by
boasters of science, humans of discipline

Water like a sea as storied
by painters of verse and tale

Water like a wave, like a mine
a humbling, turning shrine
to bravery and scare

How the water turns to Ocean
in the tides of our minds

is how you turn your palm toward
and then against

the anger of the wind, the patience of the sun

A Colony of She's

A moon like a proudly shunned sister
sits throned by the cold black
with bright dead stars as her guards

An air that is not the night herself
but doubles after day
so secrets may be seen
as frosty breath rises just above the sea

A wave as distinct from the still ocean
as a daughter from a mother;
a reckoning of water's new purpose
under the allure of the moon

A sand, an almost helper and
a billion infants of time,
arriving and loosening at the will of
the moon and the air and the waves and

my feet, two moving vessels
finally still on the shore,
finally sure of the She
they share with the matron sea

A Question Posed Against the Sea

A halting sunwise anxious
a voice thrown silent
by the crushing tide
a twice-pooled moon about
and
a damn sharp shell

A howl like envy
gone empty
a hell like inner shift child
a whisper wanting sons

The sky tells the same stories
every black night

The moon mothers the sea
like a double daughter gone amiss

The frequent becomes forgotten,
an estimate becomes a truth and

the water splits into
a thousand grand and tiny misfits,
questions posed against the sea
since time got wet and
humans peopled themselves
to the point of no return

How the Sea Knows When to Give a Hint

How the sea becomes an answer
like grandmother pulling passion tight
around your neck and releasing reason
from your wrists

How is not for us

When a breathing empty
takes to the salt and the song

The sun plays tricks:
by pulling straight the strings of mighty diamonds
that we call light
amidst the wind and wet

When a breathing empty
quivers demands

The water parts ways with direction
and delivers electric amnesty
for past transgressions

And the empty, she is filled
with breathless

A Bird, Once

To be true, this is a tale of wings

To be just, the water laps all manner of species
In the same gentle terrible way
that says, *come—*
You are safe if the winds deem it so
You are living if the waves draw your sadness
through pores opened by salt air
You are forever if you leave a memory
and pluck a shell

To be clear, a bird is an enviable power over Ocean
and the women who haunt her

a winged soft filthy song, a taster
of below with the privilege of above,

But to call it evil is to neglect
to witness the human,
the allowed developer
of inhospitable surrounds
who seeks, even so,
the not warm comfort of a shore
where answers are sought

A sea where yesterday
was never and
tomorrow is hunted

How Wise

How wise the ponderous night when not troubled by thought
How like steel, but gentle and song

An erotic species, to be clear, is an agony for *place*
a mood for populating odd tender

Children raked across hot boredom
make a god of cold clever

A moon against reason
or a hammering distance like
from here to horizon
is where I really am

A remarkable bough
a branch that bathes
its non-native bark
awaiting its fate indoors:

South sands are claimed by promise
while tidal notions are laid out across
the man-weathered table by
sheets and sheets of accident

No hints of helpable horizon
No remorseful banqueting

An indecent rape that troubles stars
(light that is technically dead)
life that was never so technical
is a perishable fault

A Known

A known is a bludgeoned human mystery.

The humor of the moon is feeling wanted yet shining alone.

The trickery of the sea is not the riddle of the sand but the hardship of the surf at play.

The courtesy of the day and the greatest allowance of the sky is a cloud
that papers the sun just so.

Time can go on as unplanned while
the secrets of an ill-conceived heaven
are visible to the kind and ruined gazers

whose stares seek up and up.

These gazers are titans of thought

these thoughts are great agents of natural disaster.

The Sea as a Useable Surface

A bottle with a message
set against the frock of sea
A secret and an answer
lost but once, now sailing free

A boat that terribles horizons
a speeding throttle: west
Eagerness at leaving
a palette foamed in jest

A ship that carries duty
a heaviness made light
by passing over salted
and exchanging day for night

*Then torrentially our fates are fed
and daring turns to drizzled dread*

A beauty that's complaining
of our fair extraction rights
a nuisance worth abating, we moan *storm*
and norm the bite

of nature well abused

Time betters few, and
humans, twice excused, find

the ocean sleeps off course, instead

Boast

For all that is boast
in the waves cooled at coast
and blued by fresh day
(night aids only gray)

For all that is true
in agitations of blue
astonishment waits
in lights prone to bright quake

For all that won't quit
as rough surf pulls and spits
for all who are tamed
by lessons unnamed

For all that's profound, in earth as on ground
For all that we sage, through riddles and age:

There thrones the sun, here sits the sea
between is spun
within is me

A Love

Found! The holiest of want
the metal bones of crave
The answer in the asking
The flesh in roads less paved

A love a love a love
A gathering of strays
A love a wand a dove
A tribe of errors saved

Unbalanced dusk or day
Uncharted, open sea
Nearly washed intention
Hopes permeating clay

A rhyme not toppled under
just paced and placed away
A love a jump a harm
A movement striking stray

A home a love a fist
A fight for perfect bright
A home a turn a tryst
Let's plainly tempt the night

A lesson less one love
A syllabus unlearned
A worded, perfect base—
let's tame and seed this place

Unrequited

Your kisses came
like a slingshot of fancy order
groundbreaking, reproachful

Excited more by an undoing than a giving, I
took your mouth in
held prisoner your fate
as your unguarded hearts claimed course
against the rush of tide
against the hush of wind

A woman is an excellent trap

Coastal Marriage

Beneath this skin is another
skin not

muscle no—nerves are yes
with chamber-charged flow
Who are these atoms at the edge

of my fingertips grazing
your face (gray
in the furry grace in the

ambling, stumbling space
between: !)

These atoms like particles
undefined
by science or love or
the two intertwined

Is knowing not seeing
the faults in the sky

Is sewing knots freeing
be bound, be at ease

When bigger words bark
the little mouths breathe

In pours the out and
brief is the tide

When woman becomes man
and girl becomes bride

A Memory of the Moon and Your Mouth

The moon was hate
the stars were young
the air was bait
for lover's tongues

The soft, the fury
it suddens past
the gates too old
to perfect last

I hold the night
its steel, its edge
I harbor solemn
my greatest dread:

That hands I grasp
enclosed by mine
are horror true
and narrow wise

are perfect anger
against the tide
of stories old, of lover's lies

Daughter

I feel my stomach is stretched over a captive moon
yet I diffuse no lunar glow, only
the pale black of the night as I push
my wonders against the wind over the sea:

Are you the reason why pink achieves against me?

Are you bent in the long, favored in the ever?

Are you the freshest of mystery but the closest of heart?

Are you a stretched and simple palette of my own complexity?

Are you an honor against the grain of dreams widowed by ambition?

*Are you made in a chamber that churns with hope and maybe, maybe
something else, something a who*

*someone a how
some fit of fancy of biology and female time?*

I feel you push back from within
and my thoughts
like worried guards
sail back to me

Sand Castles

I'm aware of my hands
as they plough through
the angry little city
you built on discrete and ponderous
dreams and sand

Castles without the dignity of purpose
or the pledge of permanence

You ask me to destroy
the toxic band of spirits
you've locked in the crumbling structures
infant fears masquerading as farce

I'm mother and murder
for you is my why
I can sport a taking away
of what pales you

And still the waves show off
a strength mightier than mother
this is the brutal crystal we avoid:
our love is greater than the speed of our fists

The Waves, They Pardon

We trail the side of evening
and walk down to the beach
The ailing light spits fresh visions as
we become a portrait
for the sun's rigorous setting

My family glows
a fetched abstraction of my perfect dreams
set at play against
the startling soft green of high tide

The wind tenders my ear
tells me I've settled and I don't deserve
the science or the hope of permanent love
tells me my partner is an unsound beast

I'm happy to hear
what I've always known—

How gentle devils can clever themselves
out of the spiced space between
a stormy lover and his favorite intrusion
is an understood mystery

A Storm

The storm adjusts itself and the pebbles children mine for
are sent off to the turbulence of tide

The soaking misdemeanors of a sea aggrieved, and all I can
see are the best boats in your shipyard,
tendered away and unavailable

All I can hear are your parting words,
phrases worked under the toast of the sun and
the cool dis-ease of a still coastal day

Yours is a language of charity and yet
I cannot help feeling like I've been robbed

The lifeguard rushes my side, he looks
troubled and I cannot hear his voice, only
the cackle of a frozen mood made public—
the storm is speaking now

A Growing Is a Gone

Stand at a distance from the death of the sea
and you will find it is the beginning of the sky

Hand off tradition and fly like a seagull
divorced from the shore
from the sunset, as
it ruins the black line called horizon

Distance is precision but we must first be looking

A strange fulcrum of chaos
emerges like a glamorous antagonist

ready to consume in a way that
is more inclusive, less coercive

As the hurricane flushes the beach with
charmless unfeminine demands,
I see she is moving and moving and
I am still standing, poised and ready and
for the first time in my life I am moving
at speeds of still, and I am going

as I've always been

About The Author

Virginia Petrucci is a writer and artist from coastal California and a former columnist for the *L.A. Post-Examiner.* Her fiction and poetry have appeared in several print and digital publications including *Flash Fiction Online, Flash Fiction Magazine, Mom Egg Review, Another Chicago Magazine,* and *Best New Writing.* Her debut chapbook, *Recipes and How-To's,* was released through Red Flag Poetry in 2017. She lives in Ventura, California with her family. She blogs at www.virginiapetrucci.com

Headmistress Press Books

She/Her/Hers - Amy Lauren

Spoiled Meat - Nicole Santalucia

Cake - Jen Rouse

The Salt and the Song - Virginia Petrucci

mad girl's crush tweet - summer jade leavitt

Saturn coming out of its Retrograde - Briana Roldan

i am this girl - gina marie bernard

Week/End - Sarah Duncan

My Girl's Green Jacket - Mary Meriam

Nuts in Nutland - Mary Meriam, Hannah Barrett

Lovely - Lesléa Newman

Teeth & Teeth - Robin Reagler

How Distant the City - Freesia McKee

Shopgirls - Marissa Higgins

Riddle - Diane Fortney

When She Woke She Was an Open Field - Hilary Brown

God With Us - Amy Lauren

A Crown of Violets - Renée Vivien tr. Samantha Pious

Fireworks in the Graveyard - Joy Ladin

Social Dance - Carolyn Boll

The Force of Gratitude - Janice Gould

Spine - Sarah Caulfield

Diatribe from the Library - Farrell Greenwald Brenner

Blind Girl Grunt - Constance Merritt

Acid and Tender - Jen Rouse

Beautiful Machinery - Wendy DeGroat

Odd Mercy - Gail Thomas

The Great Scissor Hunt - Jessica K. Hylton

A Bracelet of Honeybees - Lynn Strongin

Whirlwind @ Lesbos - Risa Denenberg

The Body's Alphabet - Ann Tweedy

First name Barbie last name Doll - Maureen Bocka

Heaven to Me - Abe Louise Young

Sticky - Carter Steinmann

Tiger Laughs When You Push - Ruth Lehrer

Night Ringing - Laura Foley

Paper Cranes - Dinah Dietrich

On Loving a Saudi Girl - Carina Yun

The Burn Poems - Lynn Strongin

I Carry My Mother - Lesléa Newman

Distant Music - Joan Annsfire

The Awful Suicidal Swans - Flower Conroy

Joy Street - Laura Foley

Chiaroscuro Kisses - G.L. Morrison

The Lillian Trilogy - Mary Meriam

Lady of the Moon - Amy Lowell, Lillian Faderman, Mary Meriam

Irresistible Sonnets - ed. Mary Meriam

Lavender Review - ed. Mary Meriam

www.ingramcontent.com/pod-product-compliance
Lightning Source LLC
Chambersburg PA
CBHW072057040426
42447CB00012BB/3159